With These Hands

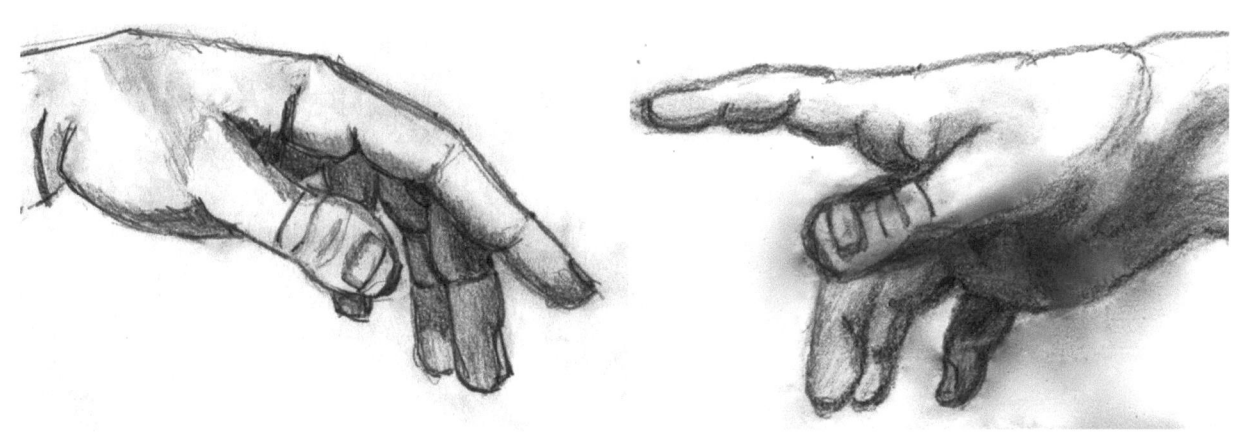

My Art, Architecture, Handcrafts, and Publications

Anton Paul Sohn

TotalRecall Publications, Inc.
1103 Middlecreek
Friendswood, Texas 77546
281-992-3131 281
www.totalrecallpress.com

All rights reserved. Except as permitted under the United States Copyright Act of 1976, No part of this publication may be reproduced, stored in a retrieval system, or transmitted in any form or by any means electronic or mechanical or by photocopying, recording, or otherwise without prior permission of the publisher. Exclusive worldwide content publication/distribution by TotalRecall Publications, Inc.

Copyright © 2025 by Anton P. Sohn MD
Copy Editor: Kristin Sohn Fermoile MD
Graphics Copyright © by Anton P. Sohn MD

ISBN: 978-1-64883-280-2
UPC: 6-43977-42802-8

1 2 3 4 5 6 7 8 9 10
First Edition

Colophon is trademarked

The scanning, uploading and distribution of this book via the Internet or via any other means without the permission of the publisher is illegal and punishable by law. Please purchase only authorized electronic editions, and do not participate in or encourage electronic piracy of copyrighted materials. Your support of the author's rights is appreciated.

ACKNOWLEDGEMENTS

Information from the following books:
1. *Idaho Wildflowers* (Greasewood Press, A.P. Sohn, 2018)
2. *With These Hands: A lifetime of Art and Crafts* (FedEx, A.P. Sohn, 2020)
3. *Pistol Creek, Idaho: History and Geography* (TotalRecall, A.P. Sohn, 2023)

"TO BUILD A BETTER WORLD"

INTRODUCTION

Following are my important accomplishments. Much of my motivation came from my mother's side of the family. My mother wrote poetry and kept a diary. Her sister, Martha Cook, had artist abilities. Not to be overlooked was my father's influence on my financial wellbeing and strength of character.

My life consisted of important evolving phases. My first interest was art, which started at approximately age ten. The second phase, woodworking, began a few years later. My interest in writing began when I was chairman of pathology at University of Nevada, Reno School of Medicine.

Motivation came from experiences in grade school #57. My art teacher, Martha Barber, encouraged my artistic abilities, and shop teacher Hershel Whitaker stimulated my woodworking interests.

In Howe High School, I decided to pursue in a career in architecture. After graduation from high school and two years (1953-55) of architecture at the University of Cincinnati, my interest career changed. I transferred to Indiana University to pursue a career in medicine. In the following chapters, I will enumerate my art, architecture, handicrafts, and publications.

NAME INDEX

NAME	PAGE
APS (Anton Paul Sohn)	2, 26, 34, 37, 52
Barber, Martha	v
Father (my)	v
Martha (Martha Cook)	v
Sohn, Arlene	52
Sohn, Eric	52
Mother (my)	v
Sohn, Kristin Fermoile	41, 52
Sohn, Kerry	37, 46, 52
Sohn, Peter	38, 52
Sohn, Phil	42, 52
Sohn, Sierra	52
Sohn, Isabella	52
Sohn, Alex	52
Sohn, Brady	52
Whitaker, Hershel	v

—IT DOESN'T GET ANY BETTER—

INDEX	PAGE
ACKNOWLEDGEMENTS	iv
INTRODUCTION	v
NAME INDEX	vi
MY ART	1
ARCHITECTURE	27
HANDCRAFTS	34
PUBLICATIONS	47
IMPORTANT LIFE EVENTS	52

MY ART

14" x 22" (WATERCOLOR)

12" X 6" (CHARCOAL)   8" X 12" (WATERCOLOR)

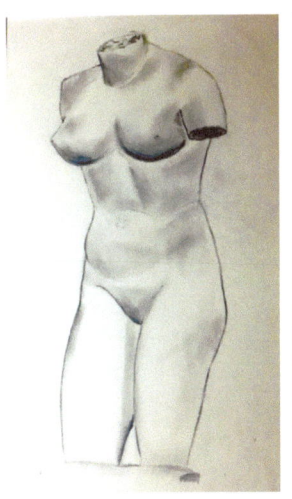

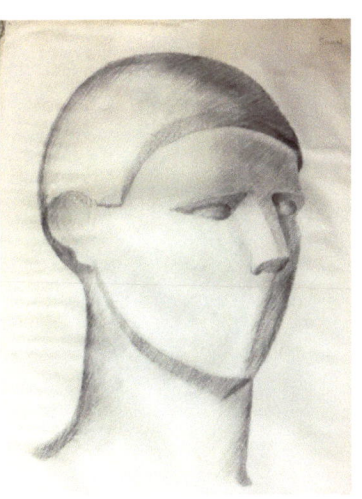

12" X 6"   12" X 9"   12" X 6"
             (PENCIL, 1954)

POSTER, LITTLE "500" BICYLE RACE, APS, IU, 1955   **4" X 8" (WATERCOLOR)**

12" X 18" CHURCH DESIGN (PENCIL, 1953)

MOUNT RAINIER, 1965 (OIL) 9" X 12"   TREES AT BACK FENCE, 1965 (WATERCOLOR) 14" X 22"

14" X 22"
GRAND CANYON, 1955 (OIL)

14" x 22" ITALIAN RIVIERA, 1953 (OIL)

18" X 12" (WATERCOLOR)

12" X 9" TREE MOLD (WATERCOLOR)

12" x 18" TREE IN SNOW (WATERCOLOR)

14" X 22" MOUNT RAINIER, 1965 (OIL)

12" X 9" (OIL) 18" X 10" (PENCIL)

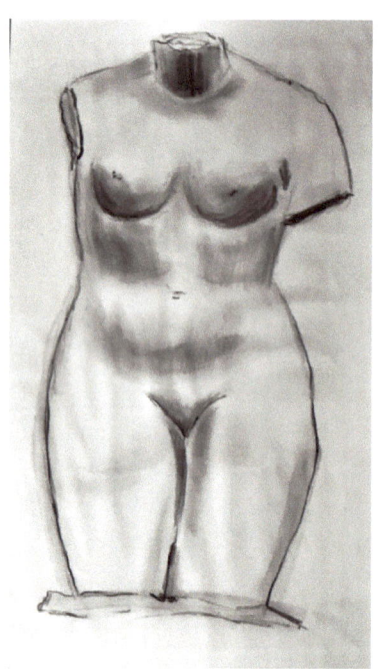 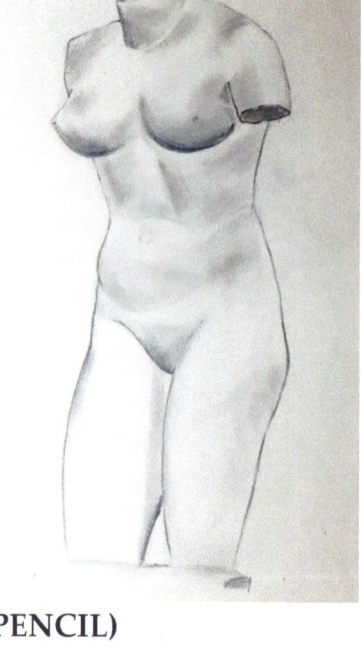

24" x 12" (PENCIL)

9" X 12" (WATERCOLOR) 9" X 12" (WATERCOLOR)

EXTERIOR PERSPECTIVE

SOUTH ELEVATION

NORTH ELEVATION

HOME DESIGN

12″ x 18″ (OIL)

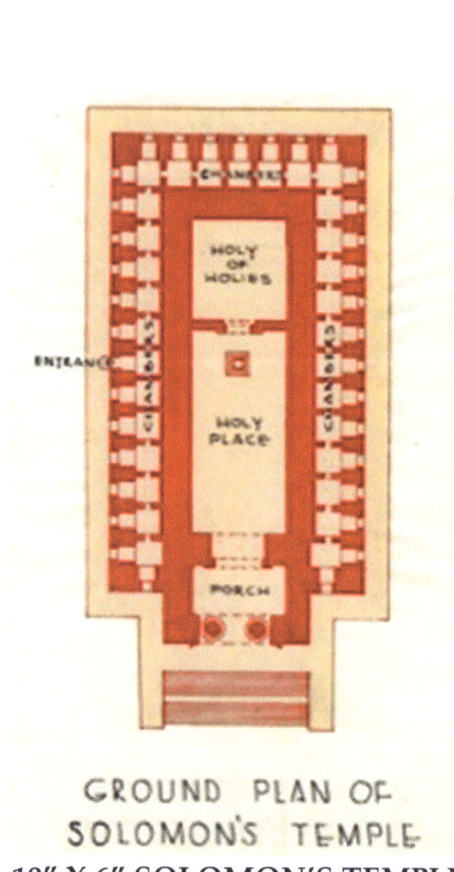

10″ X 6″ SOLOMON'S TEMPLE

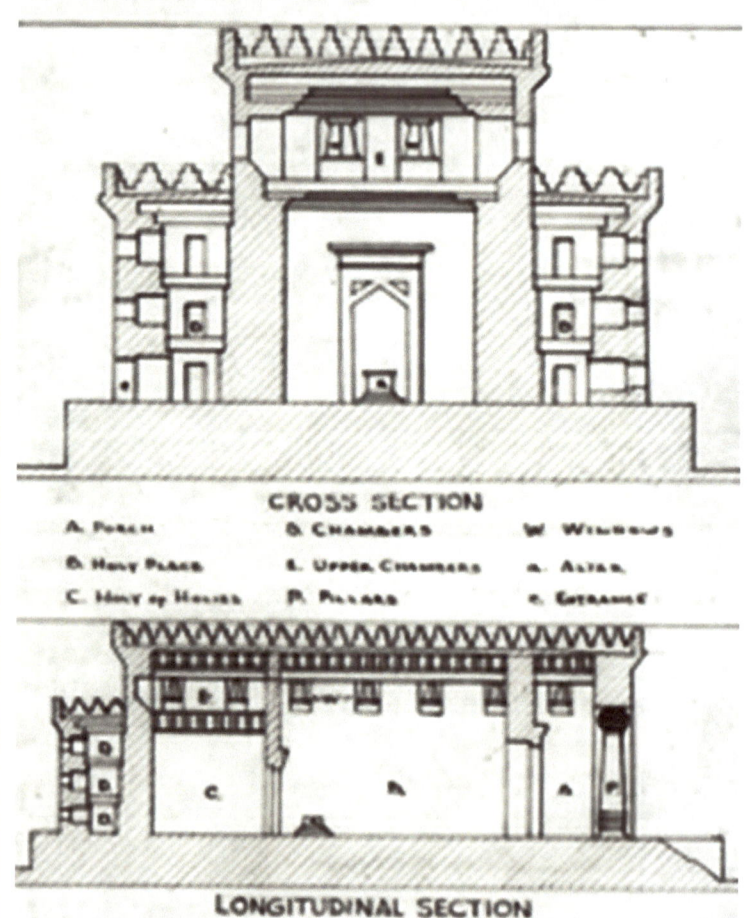

12″ X 9″ (SOLOMON'S TEMPLE)

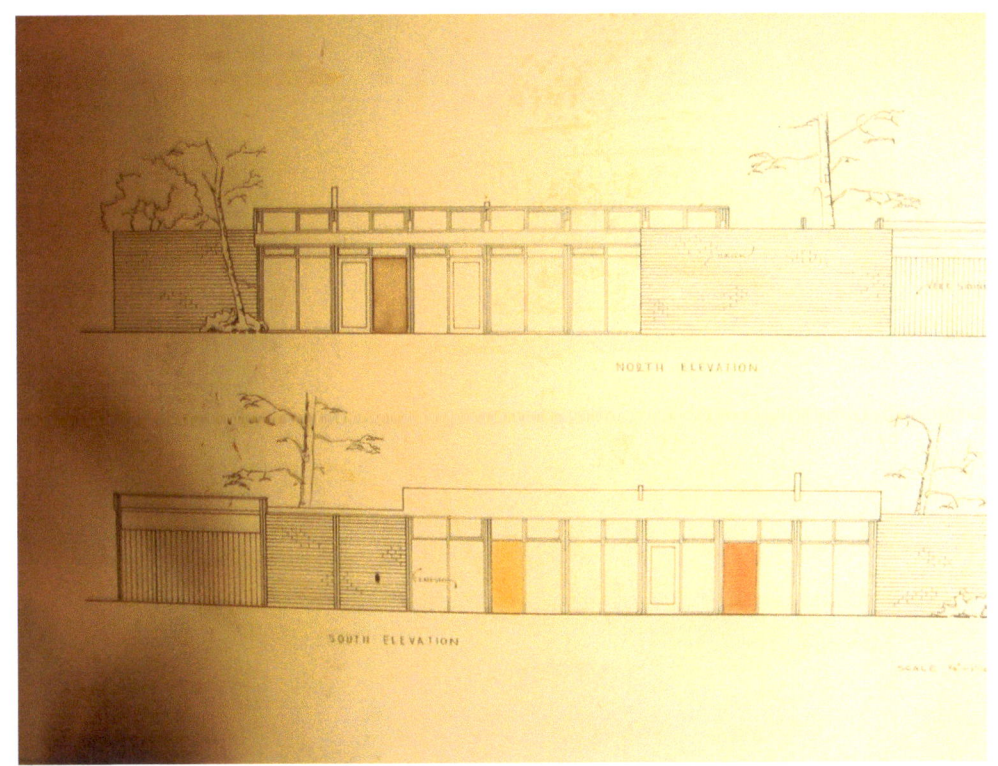
12" x 18" (HOME DESIGN) SMOKE DAMAGE

12" X 18" (HOME DESIGN) SMOKE DAMAGE

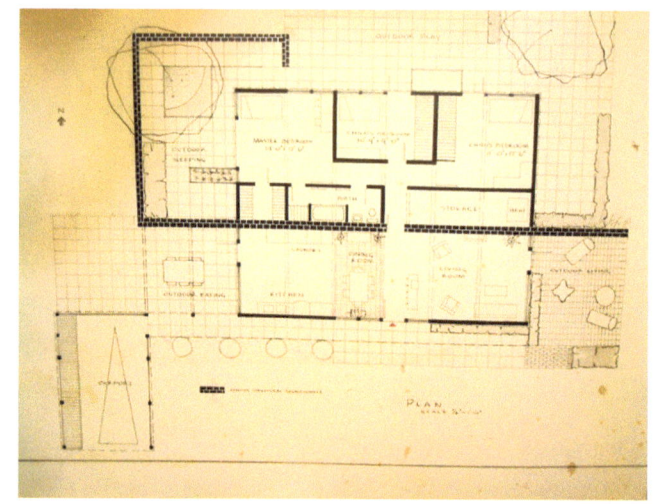

12" x 18" (HOME DESIGN) SMOKE DAMAGE

12" x 9" (OIL painting)   **12" x 9" (painting)**

9" X 12" (WATERCOLOR)

12" X 12" (WATERCOLOR)   48" X 30" (OIL)

12" X 18" (WATERCOLOR)

12" X 9" (WATERCOLOR)   12" X 9" (OIL)

12" x 20" (WATERCOLOR)

12" X 9" (OIL)   12" X 9" (OIL)

12" X 18" (WATERCOLOR)

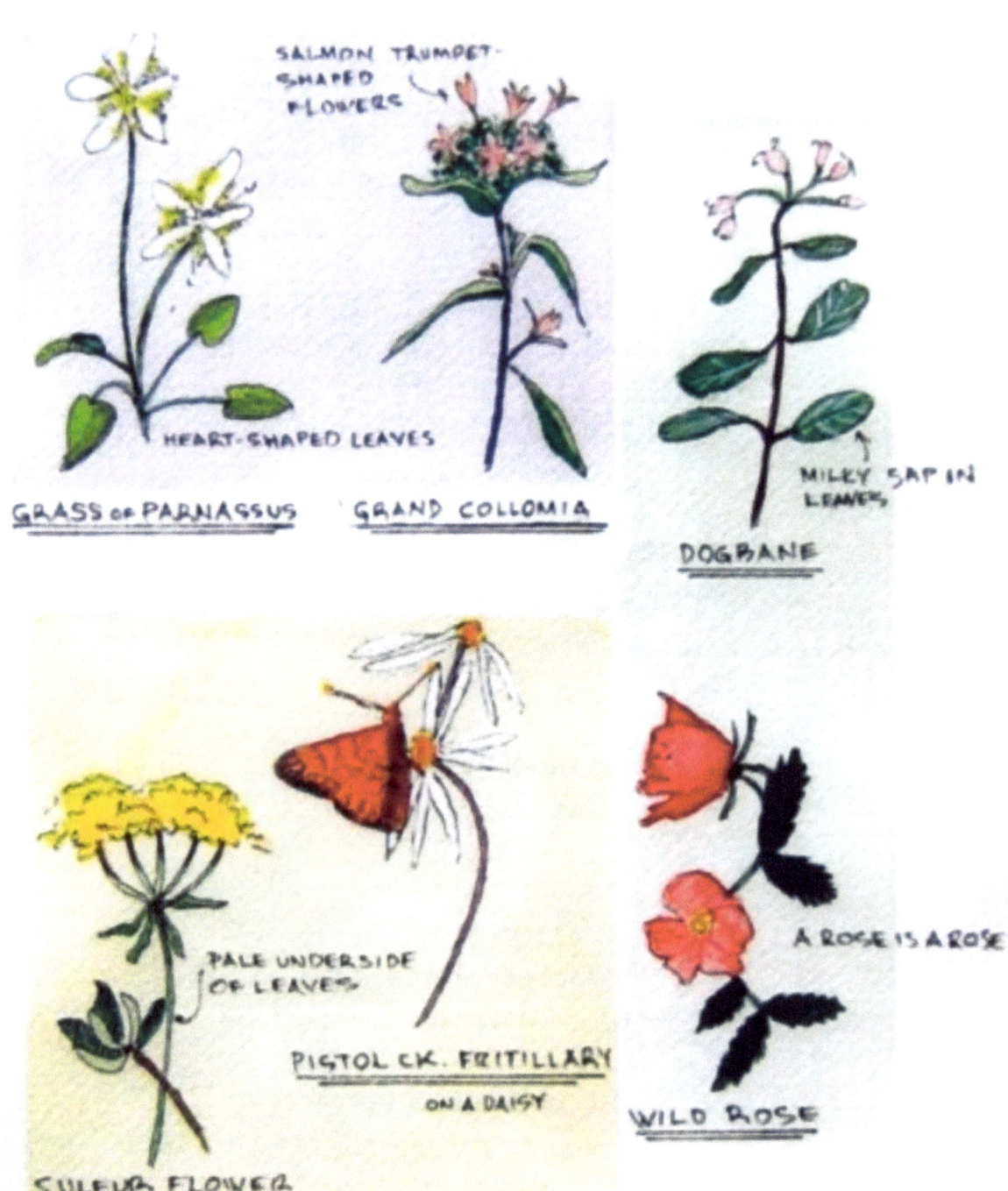

PISTOL CREEK WILDLIFE

(WATERCOLOR)

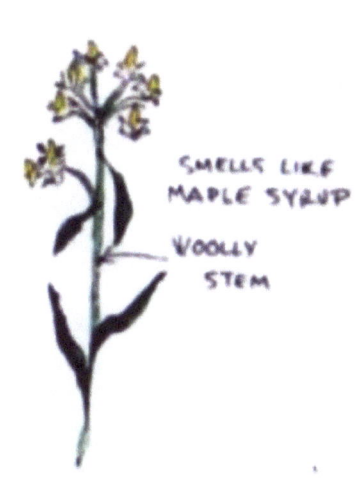

WHITE FLOWERS PL. 1

(WATERCOLOR)
PISTOL CREEK

(WATERCOLOR)

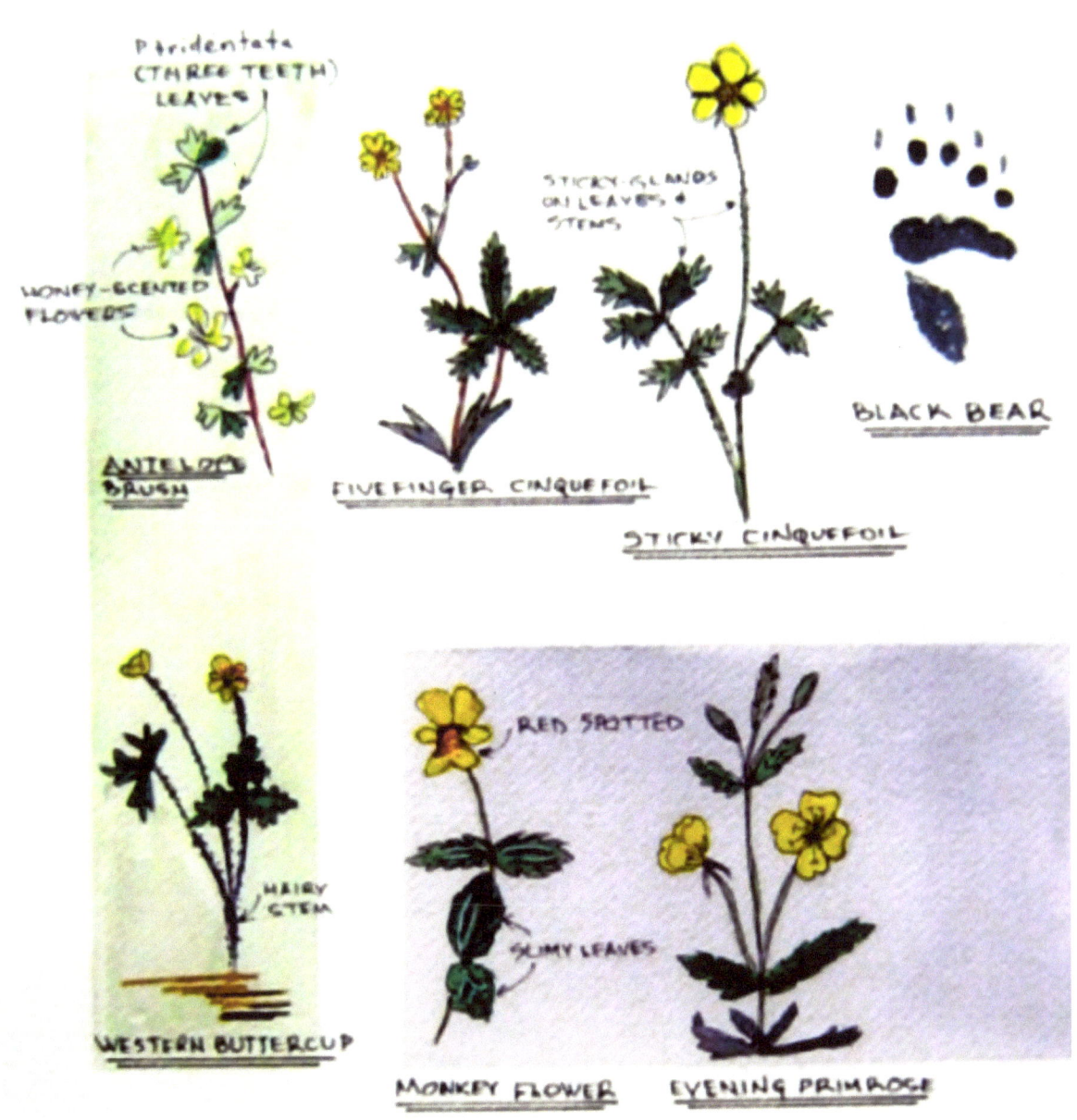

YELLOW FLOWERS Pl. III

(WATERCOLOR)
PISTOL CREEK

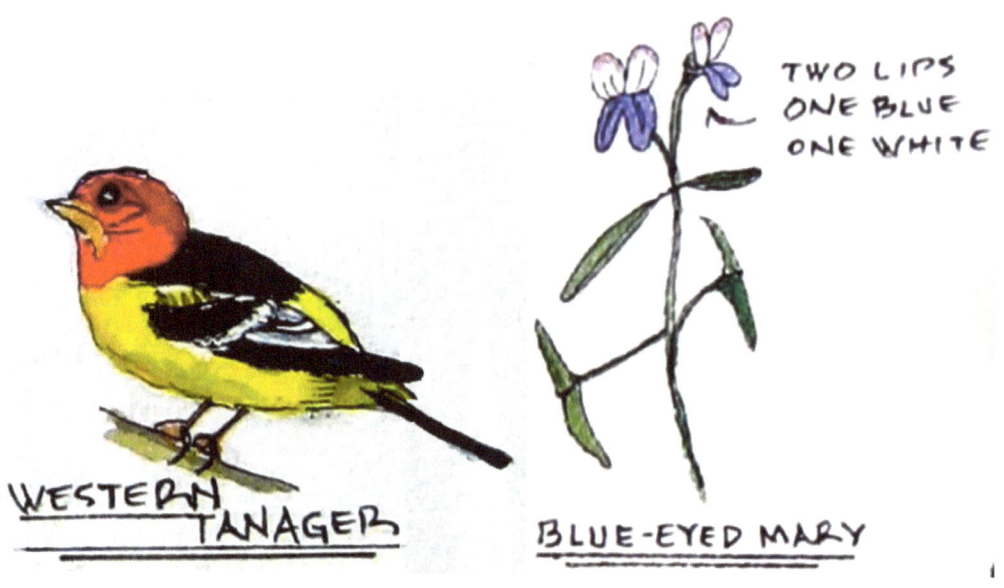
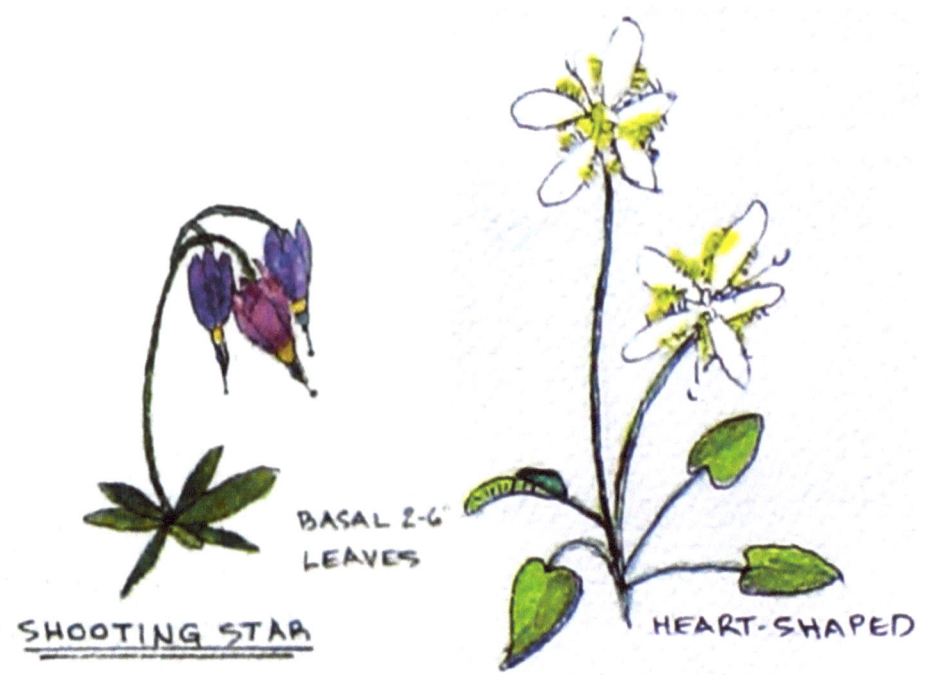

(WATERCOLOR)
PISTOL CREEK

PISTOL CREEK, IDAHO

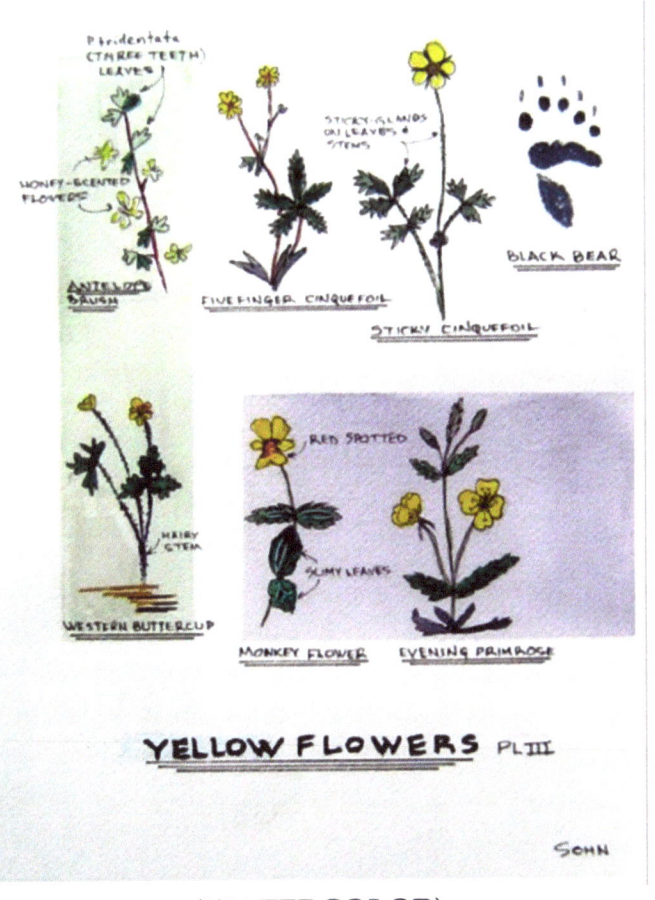

(WATERCOLOR)
PISTOL CREEK

9" X 6" (WATERCOLOR)

WYOMING PAINTBRUSH, 12" X 8"

9" X 12" (WATERCOLOR)

BEAUTIFUL SANDWORT   SPOTTED SAXIFRAGE
10" X 8" (WATERCOLOR)

ELK IN DAISIES, 12" X 12" (WATERCOLOR)

LANDING STRIP, PISTOL CREEK, IDAHO, 12" x 30" (WATERCOLOR)

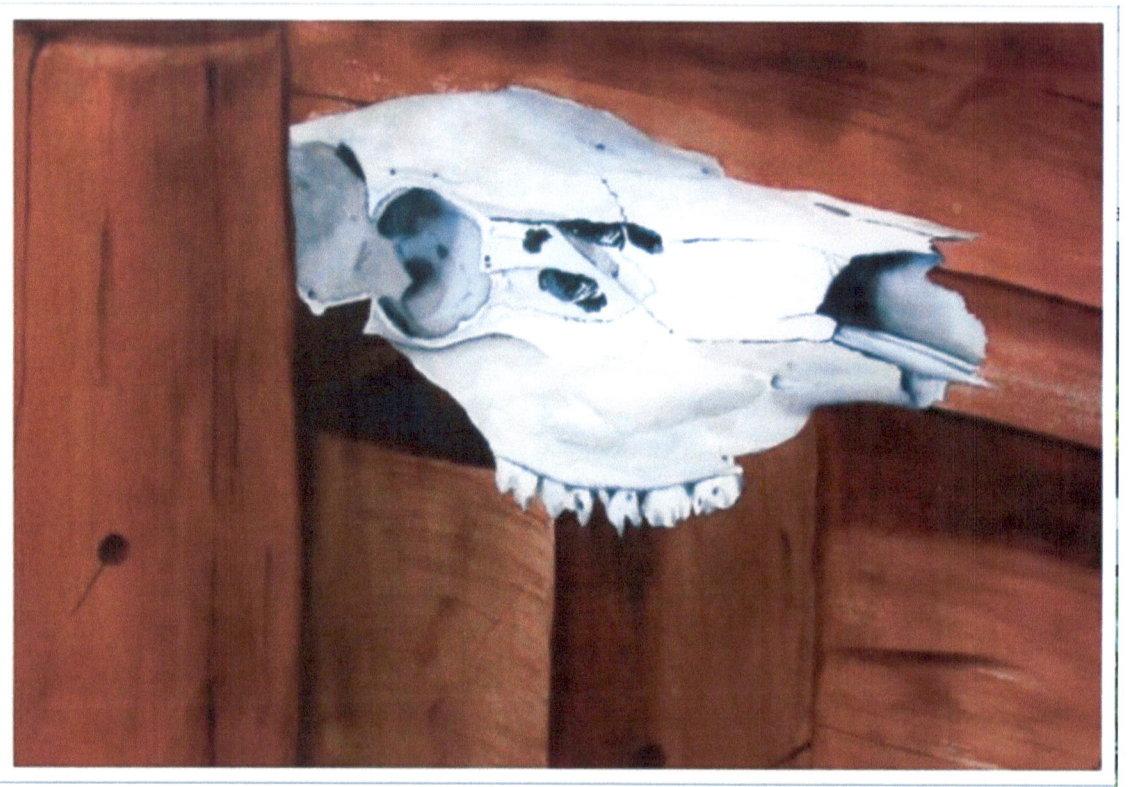
ELK SKULL, 12" X 30" (WATERCOLOR)

DONNER LAKE, 12" x 30" (WATERCOLOR)

12" X 30" (WATERCOLOR)

MY PAINTING OF MONA LISA (JOKE, JOKE)

12" X 30" (WATERCOLOR)

10" x 10" (WATERCOLOR)

MASSACHUSETTS, 12" X 30" (WATERCOLOR)

12" x 20" PAINTING

20" X 12" (WATERCOLOR)

1956, INDIANA UNIVERSITY, APS

ARCHITECTURE

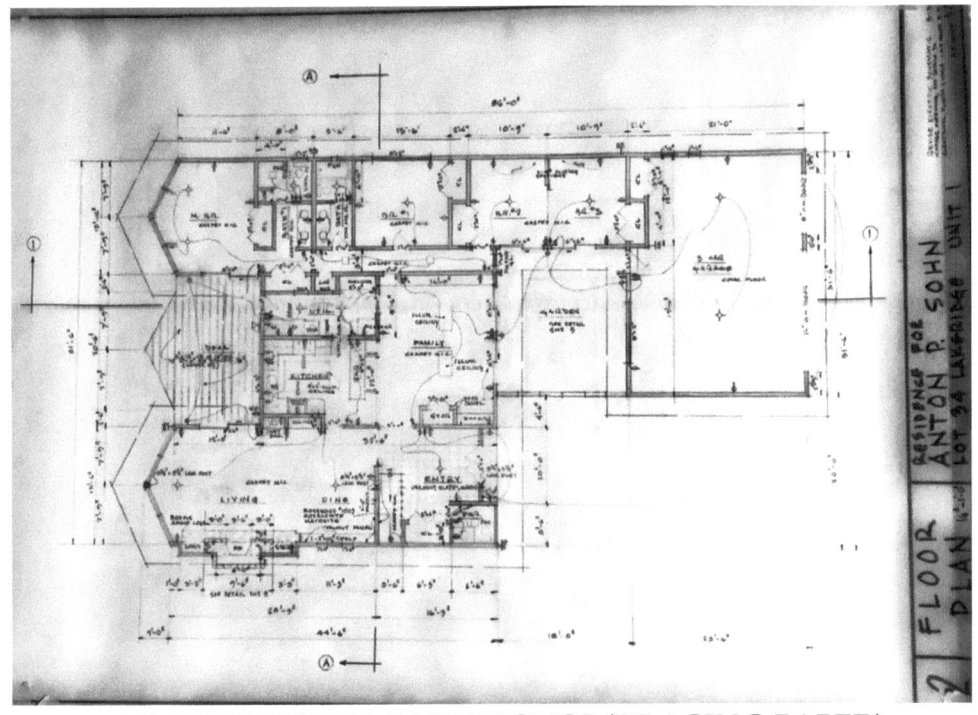

1640 MANZANITA LANE HOUSE (TRACING PAPER)

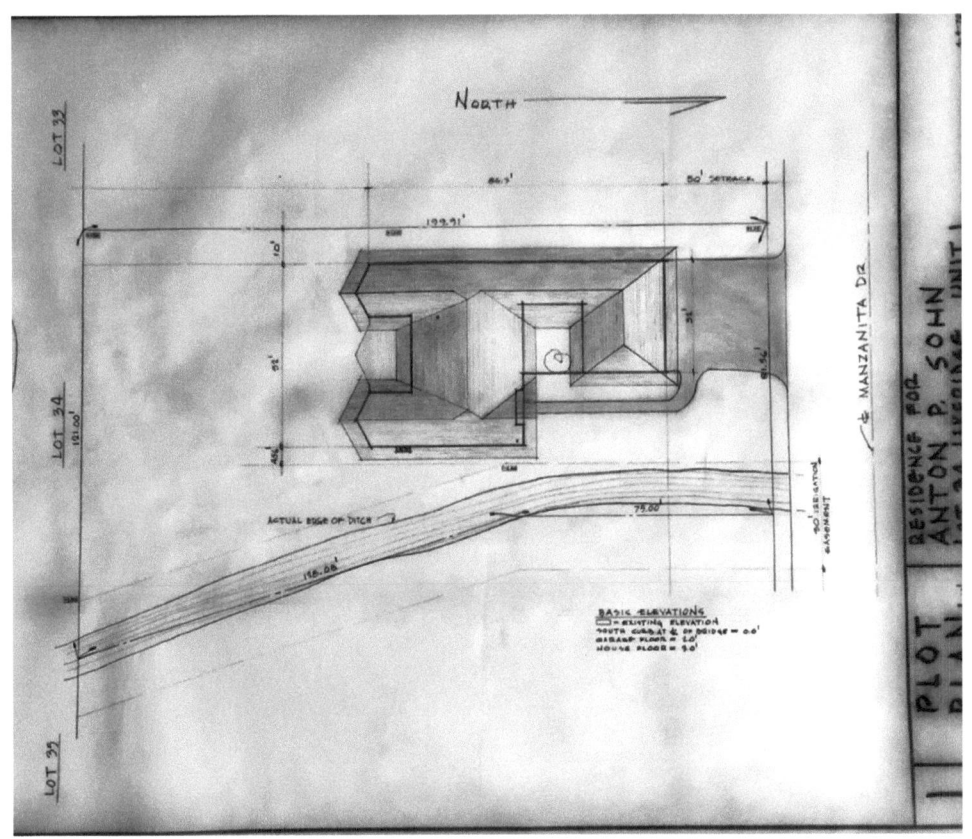

1640 MANZANITA LANE HOUSE (TRACING PAPER)

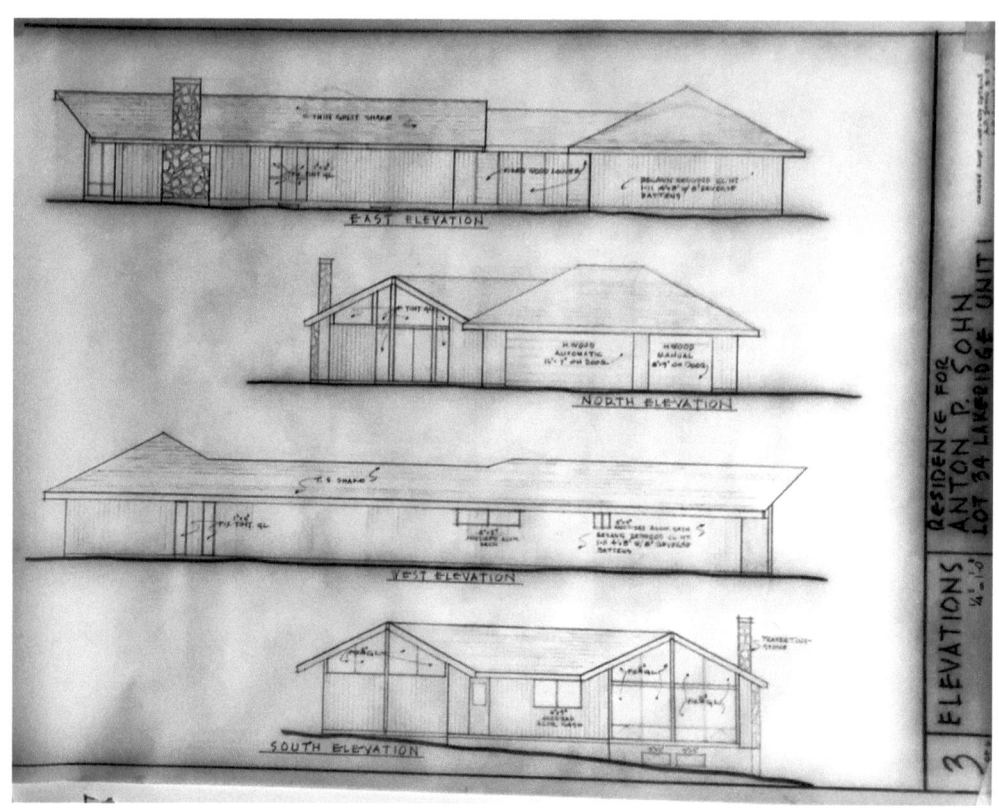
1640 MANZANITA LANE HOUSE (TRACING PAPER)

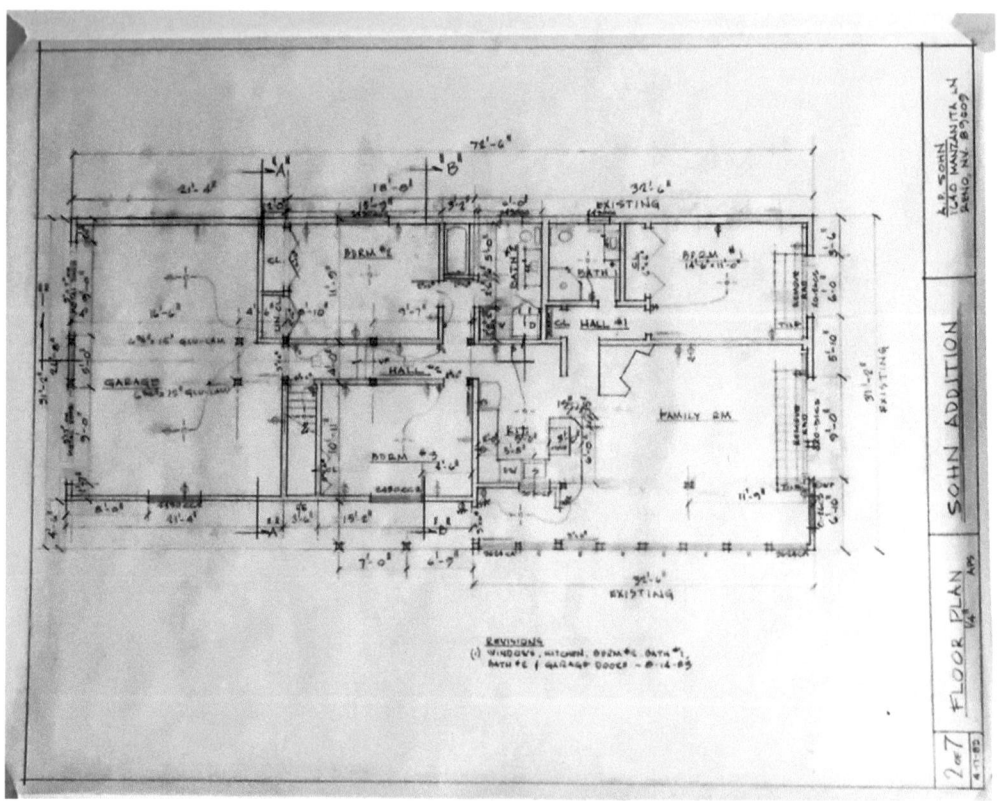
DONNER LAKE HOUSE (TRACING PAPER)

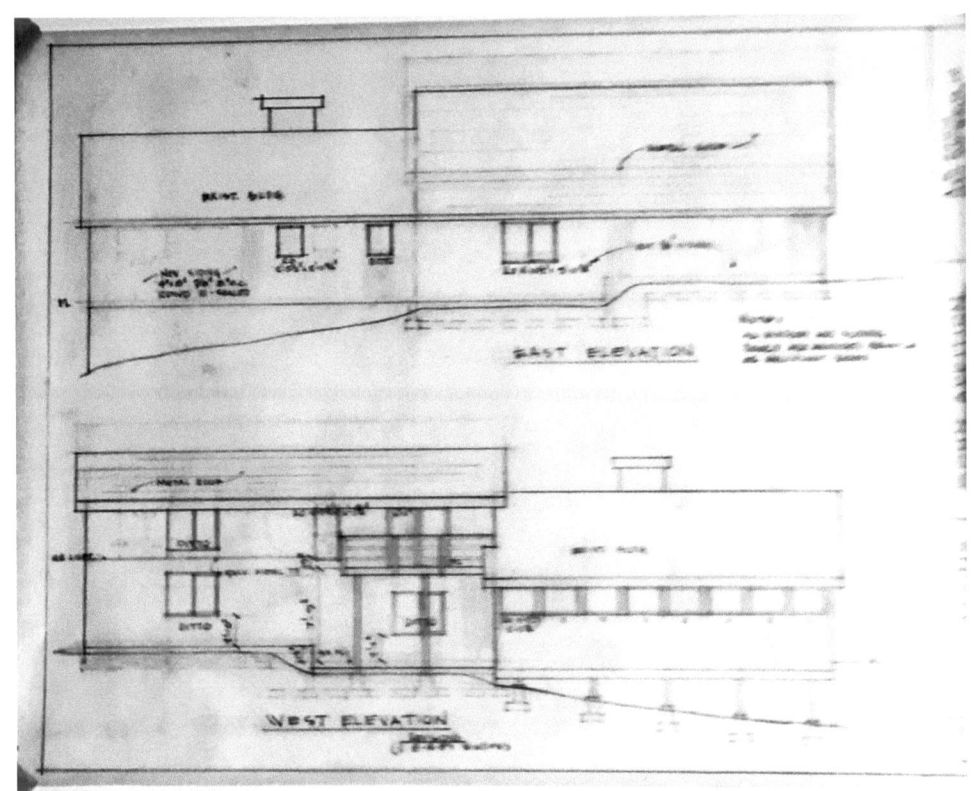

DONNER LAKE HOUSE (TRACING PAPER)

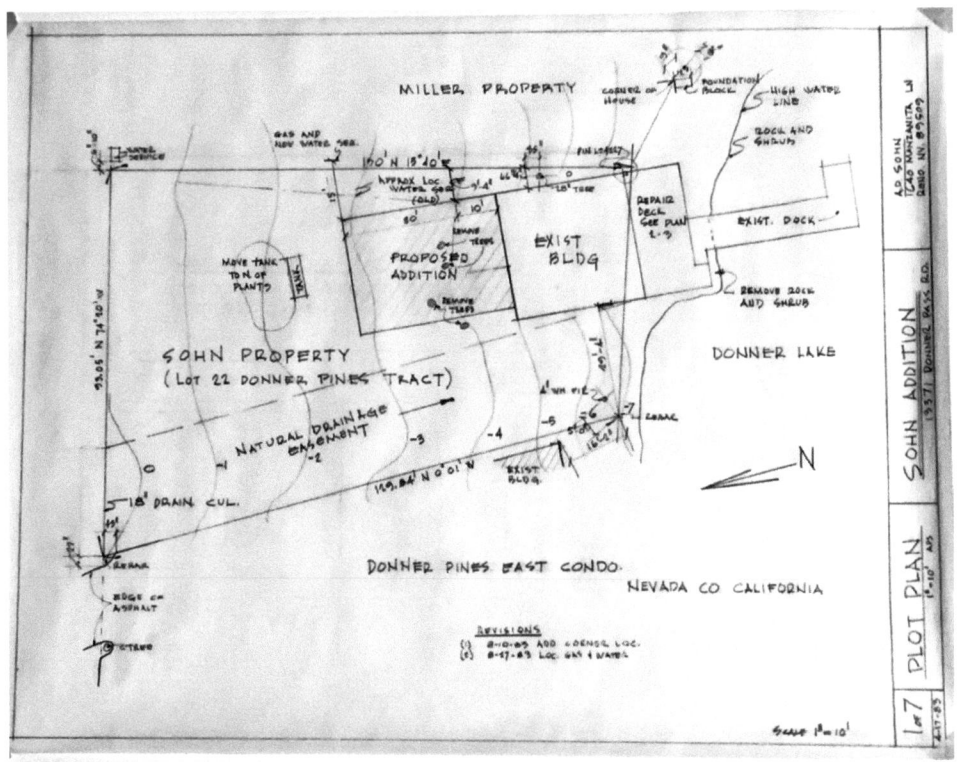

DONNER LAKE HOUSE (TRACING PAPER)

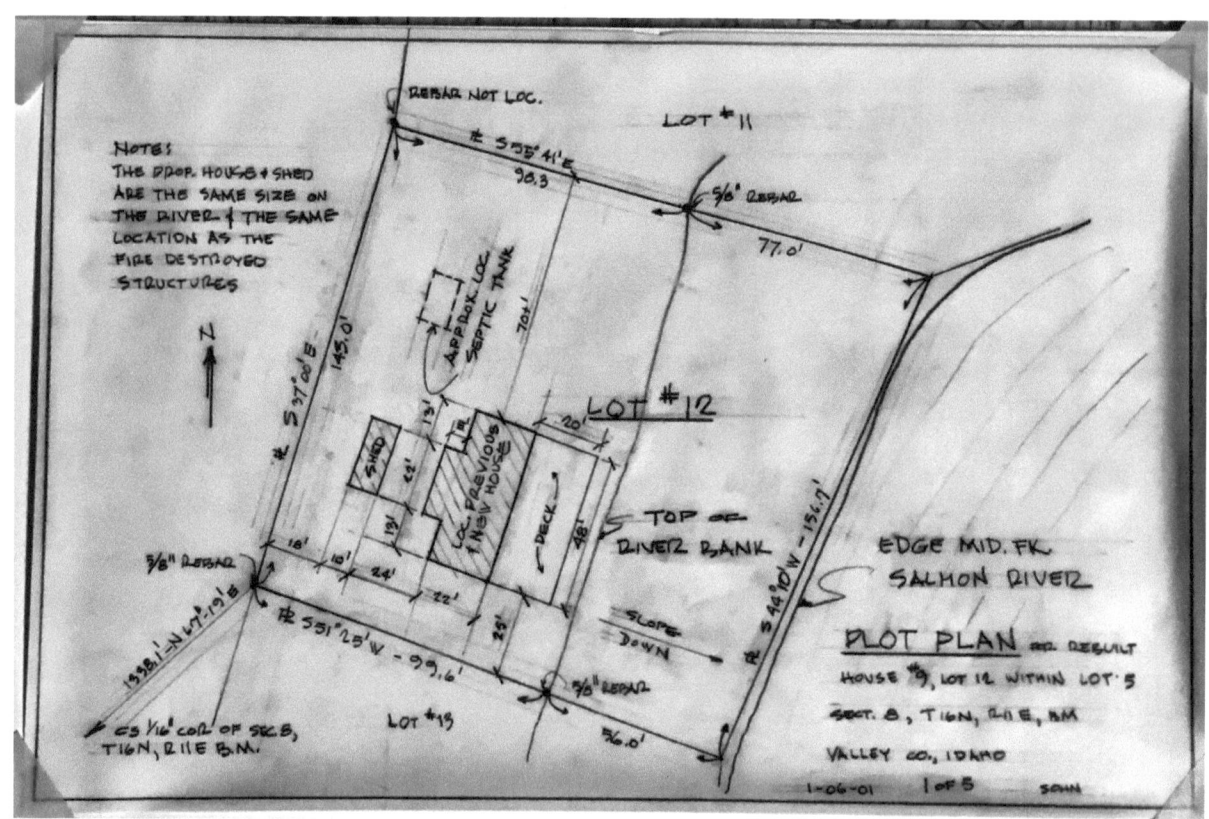

PTSTOL CREEK CABIN (TRACING PAPER)

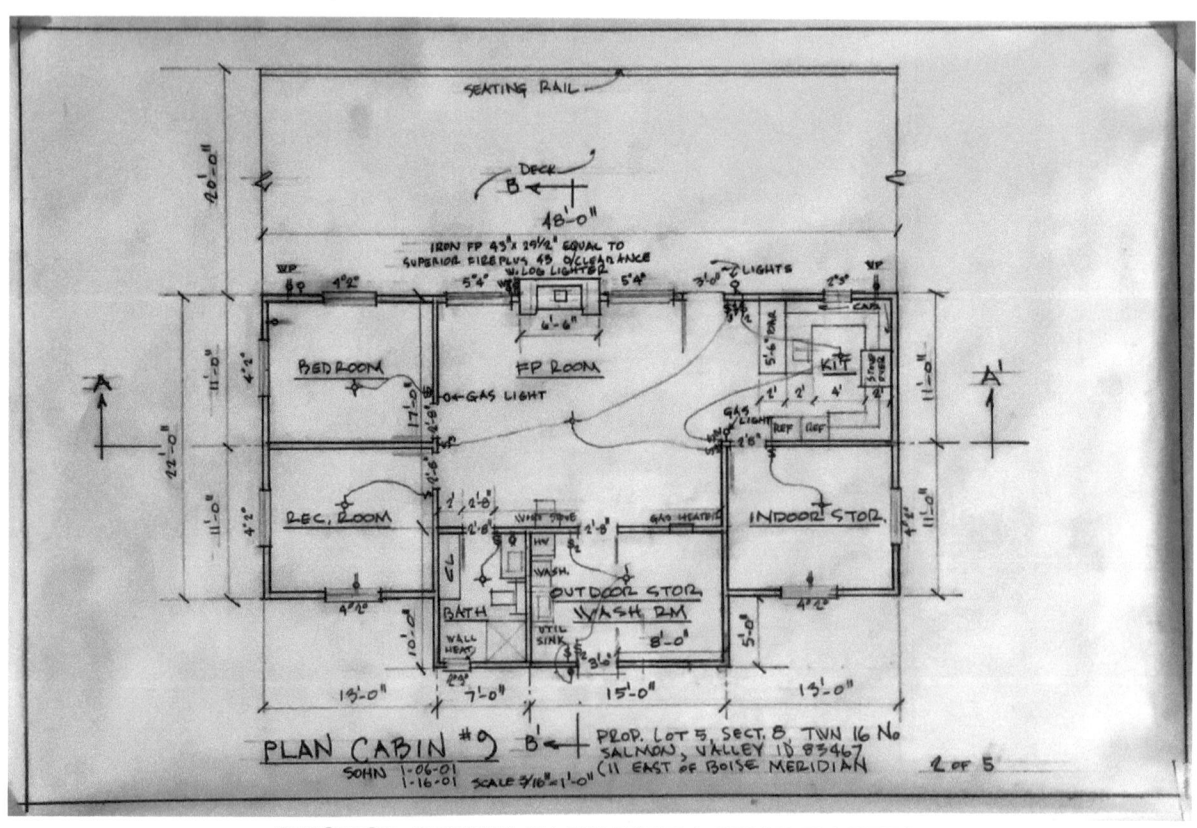

PTSTOL CREEK CABIN (TRACING PAPER)

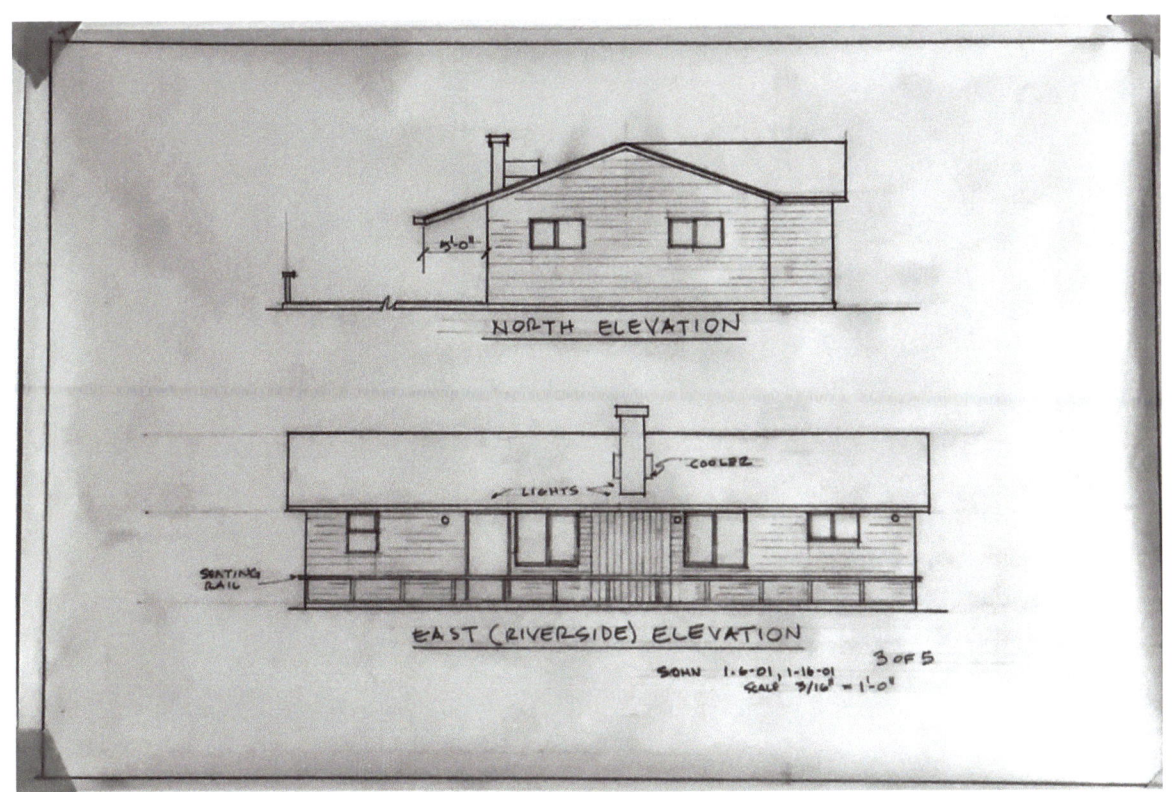

PISTOL CREEK, IDAHO, CABIN (TRACING PAPER)

PISTOL CREEK, IDAHO

CORDRY LAKE, INDIANA, CABIN

PLAYHOUSE 1640 MANZANITA

DONNER LAKE HOUSE

1640 MANZANITA LANE, FRONT DOOR

1640 MANZANITA LANE, REAR VIEW

HANDCRAFTS

8" x 12" ΦΔΘ CREST, 1956, INDIANA UNIVERSITY.
ΦΔΘ HOUSE (LINOLEUM)

1955, PLASTER SCULPTURE, APS

STAINED GLASS WINDOW, TAHOE DONNER

STAINED GLASS WINDOW, TAHOE DONNER

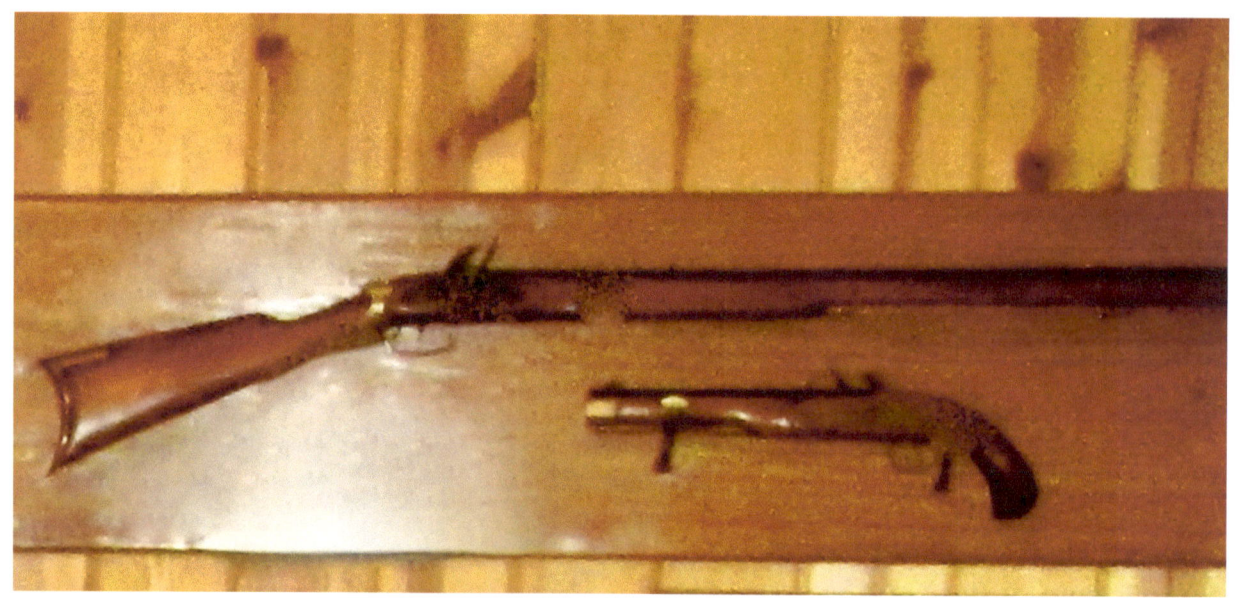

HISTORIC PISTOL AND RIFLE (MADE FROM KIT)

DEER HORNS

BENCH / FROM MANZANITA BUSH, OAK TREE, & CABNET DOOR

TABLE AT PISTOL CREEK / APS AND KERRY SOHN

BEDSIDE SHELFS.

TABLE / APS & PETER SOHN

LAMPS / FROM TREE STUMPS

8" X 10" CUTTING BOARD

TABLE / CERAMIC TILE

TABLE / OAK LIMBS & FLOOR BOARDS

SCHOOL CLOCK   CANDLE STICKS

GRANDFATHER CLOCK   WALL CLOCK

TABLES / FROM CABINET DOOR AND OAK LIMS

TABLE MADE FROM TREE

ARTIFACTS FROM DONNER TRAIL

BENCH

TABLE CLOCK

BENCH / FROM DECK BOARDS

BENCHES

DOLLHOUSE (KRISTIN'S CHRISTMAS 1978)

BENCH   **STOOLS & TABLE AT PISTOL CREEK**

CARVED DUCKS

10" CARVED INDIAN

12" CARVED BEAR

15" CARVED EAGLE

PHIL AND CARVED EAGLE

LIQUOR CABINET

BENCHS AT PISTOL CREEK

TABLES AT PISTOL CREEK

HOUSE PLAQUE   **TABLE / MANZANITA BUSH, OAK LIMBS, AND CABINET DOOR**

TABLE

TABLE FOR PRINTER

TABLE / MANZANITA BUSH
OAK LIMBS, AND CABINET DOOR

COMPUTER TABLE

LIST OF HISTORY OF MEDICINE ESSAY WINNERS

PISTOL CREEK cabin TITLE

BENCH

TABLE

TABLE AND BENCH

DONNER LAKE BRIDGE; KERRY (RIGHT) & FRIENDS

1640 MANZANITA LANE BRIDGE

PUBLICATIONS
GREASEWOOD TABLETTES

One of the most important events in my writing career was to establish a history of medicine quarterly bulletin, *Greasewood Tablettes*. Greasewood is a Nevada Great Basin plant used by Indians for thousands of years to treat disease. Dr. Owen Bolstad added the French name, Tablettes, for sophistication. Its content became the origin of several books mentioned on following pages. In addition, it became the stimulus for student research in medicine's history. At thirty-five years, *Greasewood Tablettes* is recognized as the longest continuous history of medicine bulletin in the U.S. Following is the first page of the first edition.

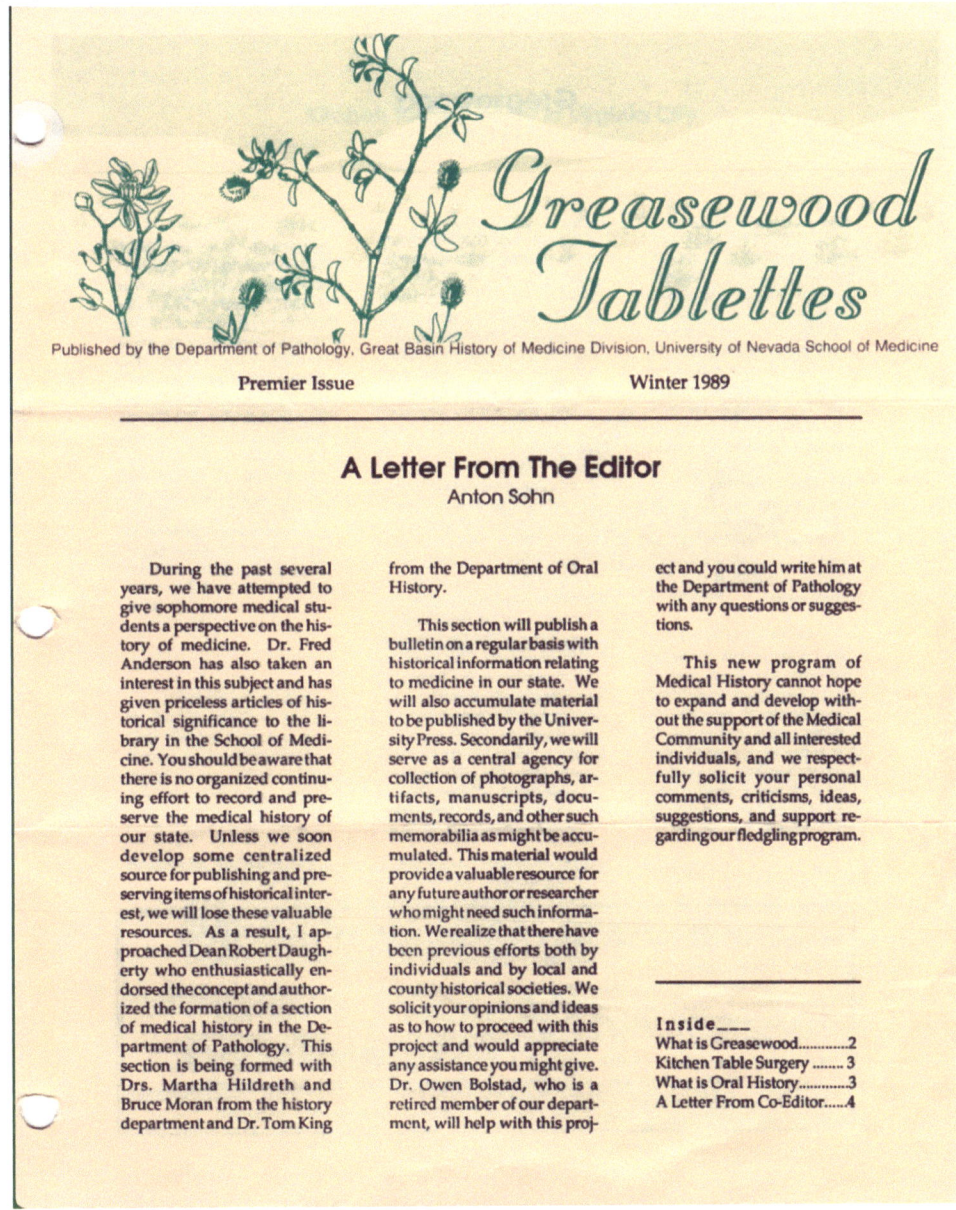

1. GREASEWOOD TABLETTES

BOOK COVERS

2. PESTILENCE, -

3. THE HEALERS, -

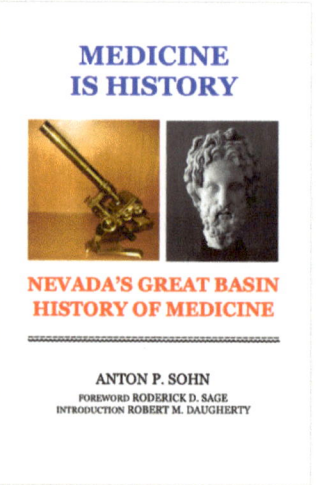
4. MED. IS HIST.

5. 150 YEARS -

6. WILDFLOWERS -

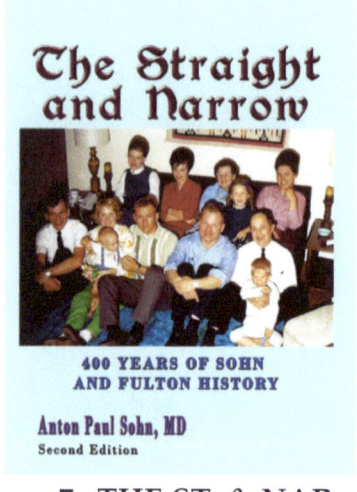
7. THE ST. & NAR.

8. KOBER -

9. NV VET -

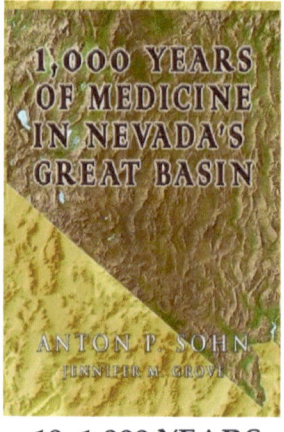
10. 1,000 YEARS -

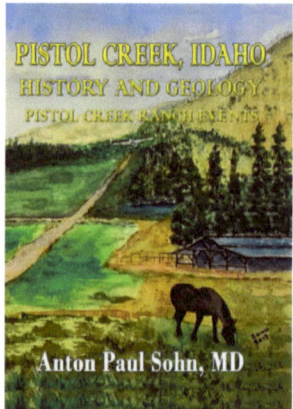
11. PISTOL CREEK

12. ID WILDFLOWERS

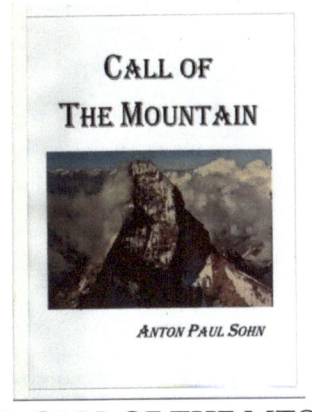
13. MY HONOR

14. CALL OF THE MTS

15. GROWING UP

16. ADDENDUM

17. TRAVELING

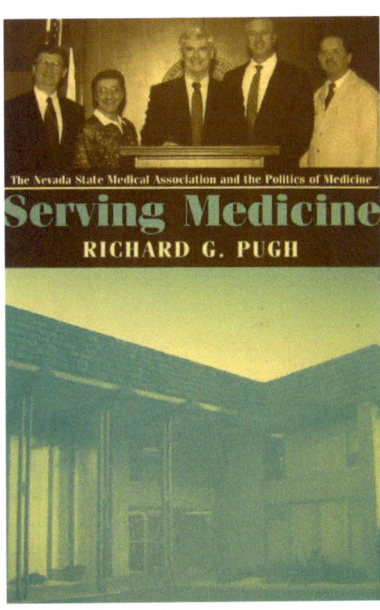
18. SERVING MEDICINE

19. SMERNOFF -

20. MOREN

21. MASSOTH

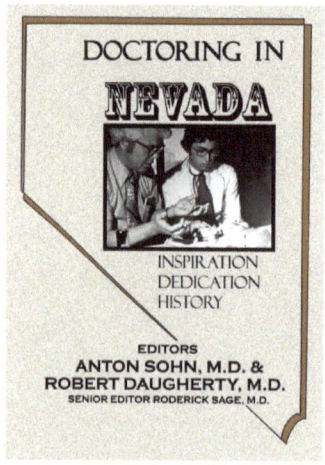
22. DOCTORING

23. CELEBRATING

24. THE CUTTING

25. PEOPLE MAKE

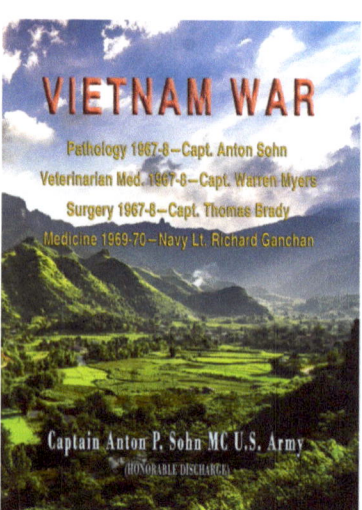
26. VIETNAM

27. BETTER MEDICINE

28. MED. IS HIST

29. THE BIRTHPLACE

PUBLICATIONS (See Book Covers)

1. GREASEWOOD TABLETTES (UNR PRESS)
2. PESTILENCE, POLITICS, AND PIZAZZ (2002, APS EDITOR, GREASEWOOD PRESS)
3. THE HEALERS OF 19TH CENT. OF NEVADA (1997, GREASEWOOD PRESS)
4. MEDICINE IS HISTORY (2017, GREASEWOOD PRESS)
5. 150 YEARS OF NEVADA MEDIVINE (2024, TOTALRECALL PUBLICATIONS)
6. WILDFLOWERS OF PISTOL CREEK (2018, GREASEWOOD PUBLICATIONS)
7. THE STRAIGHT AND NARROW (2023, TOTALRECALL PUBLICATIONS)
8. FRONTIER SURGEON, G. M. KOBER, ETC (2008, APS EDITOR, GREASEWOOD PRESS)
9. NEVADA VET. (2007, APS EDITOR, GREASEWOOD PRESS)
10. 1,000 YEARS OF MEDICINE IN NEVADA'S GREAT BASIN (2024, TOTALRECALL PUBLICATIONS)
11. PISTOL CREEK, IDAHO ETC. (2023, TOTALRECALL PUBLICATIONS)
12. IDAHO WILDFLOWERS (2018, GREASEWOOD PRESS)
13. MY HONOR TO SERVE (2021, FedEx)
14. CALL OF THE MOUNTAINS (2021, FedEx)
15. GROWING UP IN IRVINGTON (2021, FedEx)
16. ADDENDUM TO TRAVELING THE GLOBE (2021, FedEx)
17. TRAVELING THE GLOBE (2021, FedEx)
18. SERVING MEDICINE (2002, APS EDITOR, GREASEWOOD PRESS)
19. SMERNOFF (1990, APS EDITOR, GREASEWOOD PRESS)
20. MOREN (1990, APS EDITOR, GREASEWOOD PRESS)
21. MASSOTH (1995, APS EDITOR, GREASEWOOD PRESS)
22. DOCTORING IN NEVADA (2013, GREASEWOOD PRESS)
23. CELEBRATING 60-YEARS OF ARLENE AND ANTON'S FAMILY (2024, TOTALRECALL PUBLICATIONS)
24. THE CUTTING EDGE (2003, GREASEWOOD PRESS)
25. PEOPLE MAKE THE HOSPITAL (1998, GREASEWOOD PRESS)
26. VIETNAM WAR (2022, TOTALRECALL PUBLICATIONS)
27. BETTER MEDICINE (2023, GREASEWOOD PRESS)
28. MEDICINE IS HISTORY (2017, GREASEWOOD PRESS)
29. THE BIRTHPLACE OF NEVADA MEDICINE (2009, GREASEWOOD PRESS)

IMPORTANT LIFE EVENTS
Author Anton Paul Sohn MD

Born: Indianapolis, Indiana, October 1, 1935
University of Cincinnati, Architecture, 1953-55
Indiana University, B.A. Anatomy and Physiology, 1957
Louisiana State University, Fellowship, Tropical Medicine, 1960
Indiana University, M.D., 1961
San Francisco General Hospital, Intern, 1961-62
Married: Arlene Ann (Hedegard) Sohn, June 15, 1963
Tacoma General Hospital, Pathology Residency, 1963-66
Children: Anton Phillip, 1966; Eric Allan, 1969; Kristin Diane, 1971
Grandchildren: Anton Peter, 1994; Alexander Wise, 1997; Isabella Jolie, 2011;
Kerry Thomas, 1997; Brady Carson, 1999; Sierra Morgan, 2000
Board Certified in Clinical, Anatomical, and Forensic Pathology
Captain, U.S. Army, 1966-68
U.S. Army, Fort Ord, California, 1966-67
Chief Pathologist, 9th Medical Laboratory, Saigon, Vietnam, 1967-68
Bronze Star **for** Meritorious Service under Hostile Fire, Vietnam, 1968
U.S. Army, Honorable Discharge, 1968
Renown Medical Center, Pathologist, 1968-84
Renown Medical Center, Director of Labs, 1977-84
Nevada State Medical Association, President, 1984
Univ. Nevada, Reno School of Medicine: Chair, Dept. Path., 1984-2009
Johns Hopkins University, Inst. Hist. of Medicine, Research Assoc., 1992-93
Founder, Great Basin History of Medicine Museum
Founder, Greasewood Press and Quart. Bulletin (Greasewood Tablettes)
Retired 2009

MICHELANGELO'S SISTINE CHAPEL CEILING PAINTING

www.ingramcontent.com/pod-product-compliance
Lightning Source LLC
Chambersburg PA
CBHW041707160426
43209CB00017B/1773